The Prayer Pallett

Ruth Merritt

Copyright © 2024 Ruth Merritt

All rights reserved.

No part of this book may be reproduced, stored in a retrieval system, or transmitted by any means, electronic, mechanical, photocopying, recording, or otherwise, without written permission from the author.

ISBN (Paperback): 979-8-9911398-7-8
ISBN (eBook): 979-8-9911398-6-1

Introduction

It was the mid-1950s and the fall season in Greene County began cold and wet. Winter would not begin until December, but the brutal cold rain and the strong winds made late September and early October feel like the dead of winter. Cotton still lingered in the fields, but it was too cold for the cotton pickers to gather the remaining harvest. One could only hope that the sun would shine brightly over the next few weeks so that the final picking could be done. For many of the cotton pickers, the continuous rain meant no money at the end of the week. For others, who had a second income, there was just enough to get by until the next paycheck. The lack of money was hard for all families, *especially* those who had only one income. Yet, there was hope.

Nights on the inside of our house were cold. The brisk wind blew through the cracks of the floors, walls, and the old, dilapidated windows. Sometimes, it almost felt as if we were outside. Grandma would stuff the cracks of the two doors and the old windows with rags and newspaper to keep the heat from the small, wood stove inside the three-room house. There were eight of us kids and my grandma. The house was small, but she made it work. There was a strength about her that was unbreakable, unstoppable, and absolutely amazing. She knew how to take what appeared to be negative and turn it into a positive so that her family was secure.

The two beds could not hold all of us, so Grandma pulled out the pallets every night. The pallets were quilts that Grandma and her quilting circle made during the spring and summer. Colorful patches of fabric taken from old dresses, flour sacks, and leftover fabric were sewn together in beautiful patterns that each woman created. Woven into each square, triangle, and circle were stories of love and happy times, of struggles and hard times, of brokenness and hurt, of faith, hope, and trust. These stories and memories would linger for years to come. Each generation would tell the next generation about life in the years that preceded their own.

As they sewed each shape by hand, they shared their feelings of despair, their joy and happiness, their day-to-day concerns during a time when life was hard, and of course, the local gossip. Yet there was hope. The faith in this circle of women was undaunted. It was faith in their Almighty God. A faith that they had steadfastly relied on for decades. These women were warriors. No matter how difficult their circumstances were, they knew the power of faith, hope, and prayer. Most of all PRAYER! None of them knew that they had impressed upon me the need for their God and their God kind of faith...a steadfast reliance, unwavering confidence in God, his power, his love, his goodness, and his grace. They were role models for me, and the stories from their pallets live in my heart. They left a legacy and many lessons. Years after they had all left this earthly realm, many of those pallets graced the beds of their children, grandchildren, and great-grandchildren.

Their prayers, their faith, their God; thus, the need for a prayer pallet.

CHAPTER 1

Blue Quilts and Purpose

The Lord brought me to South Carolina for a purpose. He gave me a brand-new house in 2006 which made me very happy. I was beyond grateful, and I wanted to learn how to have a home in which God would be pleased to make his abode. I didn't want to even try to maintain a house without his help. I didn't just want a house; I wanted a home, and I knew that for the home to manifest, it had to start with me.

Not long after I moved to the new house, my son gave me new furniture. The delivery guys brought the furniture in and proceeded to arrange it as I instructed. As I watched them, something about the blue quilts that covered the sofas, chairs, and tables caught my eye. I remembered the quilts that my grandmother and her friends made when I was a child. I asked one of the guys what they were going to do with them and without hesitation, he gave them to me. Ah, what a beautiful gift. They didn't know the magnitude of what they had just done for me. Come to think of it, I didn't know the magnitude of what they had just done for me. Little did I know that this was the beginning of the prayer pallet experience....an experience in which I would hear God speak to me, teach me, and completely change my life. At that moment, I knew deep within me that if I were going to change, it had to begin with me. I had to have a new mindset, a new thought life (i.e., one that was focused solely on Christ), and a sincere willingness to accept what he was about to manifest in my life.

I washed, dried, and carefully folded each quilt. One day, I was studying the book of Exodus and I discovered that blue was one of the colors of the yarn that was used in the curtains in the Tabernacle and the tassels of clothing. In Exodus 26:1, God instructs the Israelites, "Moreover, you shall make the tabernacle with ten curtains of fine twine linen and blue and purple and scarlet yarns; you shall make them with cherubim skillfully worked in them." Maybe the color had a deeper meaning than what was on the surface. It did! According to Numbers 15:37-41, the Lord instructed Moses to tell the Israelites to put a blue thread in the tassels of the corners of their garments so that they would remember and do God's commandments. Well now, I took this to mean that they were to be loyal to God. So, Ruth, where is your loyalty? It would come while I was on the pallet. The blue quilts would be my place to access a deeper level in God; however, I had not discovered that realization yet. When I started to lay before him each day, I had no plan and no agenda. I had no unction of how he was going to do it, but I do know that whatever it took, I was desiring with everything in me to hear God speak to me. I placed the quilts on the floor beside my bed and for the next weeks and months, this place became my "prayer closet".

The first day I sat on the pallet before the Lord, I quietly reflected on my life. Early on, God was the farthest person from my mind and my life. Every day was full of me. I did everything there was to do and everything that I thought might be fun. I went everywhere to see and be seen. I was the people pleaser and party starter. I was confident that when I walked into the party house, it was on. "Hey, let's partay!" I was the center of attention, the comedian, and the loudest. I wasn't concerned that my life was on a downward spiral. I was going, going, going in the wrong direction on the wrong road that took me to places I didn't need to be.

What I didn't know at that time was God has a purpose for every person he created, and He alone will bring that purpose to bear. I was attending a funeral and a minister gave me 2 Chronicles 16:9 which states, "Certainly the Lord watches the whole earth carefully and is ready to strengthen those who are devoted to him. You have acted foolishly in this matter; from now on you will have war." This story was about King Asa, the ruler of Judah, who relied on man's help rather than relying on God. The prophet Hanani informed Asa that he did not consult the Lord in the matter and as a result, Asa would have war. Asa was so furious with Hanani that he had him jailed. Oh, how we act foolishly and leave God out of the matters of our lives. I wasn't happy with the word but the ironic part about it is that I *knew* that I needed more. I needed a new life, a new way of living, and a new way of thinking. My grandmother would have simply said, "You need to straighten up and fly right." I didn't want God to call me a fool because I kept doing foolish things. Yet, I left God at the place where the minister gave me the word. It wasn't enough that the minister gave me a word, but my daughter, who is now my pastor, later told me, "God is

The Prayer Pallett

not pleased with you being everywhere. He wants to use you, but you have to let Him be first in your life." Talking about a slap in the face! I heard the minister, but I didn't listen, and I certainly didn't listen to my daughter. They were my Hanani. Of course, I didn't have them jailed but I didn't listen either. I kept right on traveling the wrong roads that took me to places that were not good for me. My lifestyle felt good, and I had no intention of allowing anyone to cramp my style. I lived by my own knowledge and rules. I put God in the corner and left him there. On Sunday morning, I would pick up the "thought" of God on my way to church. I thought about him as I sang in the choir and as I said an occasional "Amen" to the preacher; however, it was all for show. I was doing a lot of singing, going a lot of places, and pretending to know God but I wasn't allowing God to truly reign in my life. I had no understanding, no true knowledge of God, no strength, and no Jesus.

I finally woke up and admitted to myself that I could change or remain the same. I *needed* Jesus to rule and reign in my life and I *needed* everything he was offering me. The eyes of the Lord searched until he found me. When the minister gave me the scripture, I didn't know or understand the meaning let alone what I was going to do with it. Deep inside my heart, there was a longing that I could not recognize or understand so I started to look closer at Ruth. I was acting like Asa. Asa heard the word from Hanani but that wasn't the only word that he heard. Azariah told him, "The Lord will stay with you as long as you stay with him. When you seek him, you will find him but if you abandon him, he will abandon you." If that word is not a wake-up call, I don't know what is. Yes, I saw Ruth written

The Prayer Pallett

all in this scripture. I had to start somewhere, and it was time. I was quickly realizing that I *had* to learn about God because he was the one who was looking to and fro to find me.

The first time I lay on the pallet, God said, "It's just Me and you. In my presence, this is the place the devil can't find you. The devil can't get in. This is the place that you meet with Me and you will find joy unlike anything else. If you want Me, I am here to help you embrace Me and trust in my perfect love and comfort. Only I can bridge that gulf of thoughts that has been taking you to a place of indecision. Now that you want it to begin with you, I have to get you focused on the One that is in control. I want you to move closer to me. With you knowing for yourself that you are in my presence, wonderful things will happen for you." Purpose— God's purpose. I remembered what my daughter said, "God wants to use you but you have to let him be first in your life." His voice was crystal clear and I didn't doubt who I was hearing. As he spoke, I focused, I heard, and I listened. Yes, I listened this time! I *wanted* God to know that I was serious, that I deeply desired to hear him and to please him with my whole heart. "God, it's me, Ruth. I want you to know I'm here. I don't want to assume anything." The realization of who I am hit me like a brick. I am created in His image and likeness, so I don't have to wonder if he is here. I can know with unwavering confidence that my loving Father is sitting on this pallet with me. That revelation was enough to shout about! I was at peace.

I often lay on my pallet and examine my life through my own lens, and I see a poor reflection of myself but the longer I think about who I am and whose I am, the guilt and shame begin to slowly disappear. I don't have to wonder *will* God answer or whether I am hearing from God. This is the beginning!

I want to know the heart of God. I need so much more of him in me than I have! He tells me how to find the healing salve that restores. When Jesus saw me lying there in a fallen and broken condition, he asked, "Ruth, do you want to get well?" You know what came to mind? Yes, the man at the pool of Bethesda. Jesus asked him the same question, "Do you want to get well?" He answered, "I can't for I have no one to help me into the pool at the movement of the water. While I am trying to get there, someone else always gets in ahead of me." (John 5:7) I was afraid to say I can't. I had lived "I can't" too long, so I said, "Yes Lord!!! Yes Lord, I want to get well!" My yes started the healing process. I *wanted* the healing to begin immediately. God is the light that I have been searching for, so I trust him to shed his divine light on *every* area of my life and restore the years that I was blind to the things of God. I am convinced now that it all begins within me.

I can now say, my entranceway is you, Lord. The unfolding of your words gives light and understanding to the simple. Direct my footsteps according to your word; let no sin rule over me. (Psalm 119:130, 133)

CHAPTER 2

Made Right with God

I committed to meeting God on the prayer pallet daily because I deeply desired to be right with God. I could not achieve this on my own. Unconfessed sin in my life, ungodly behavior, doubt, weak faith, and failure to listen to him were just a few issues that were keeping me from right standing with him. As he talks to me, I learn that I have been made right with God by faith in Christ Jesus and that faith helps me to fulfill the law of God. The Amplified version says it this way in Romans 5:1, "Therefore, since we have been justified [that is, acquitted of sin, declared blameless before God] by faith, [let us grasp the fact that] we have peace with God [and the joy of reconciliation with Him] through our Lord Jesus Christ (the Messiah, the Anointed)." Jesus made it possible for me to be restored unto God. When I accepted him as my savior, I was freed, cleared, and forgiven! Wow, his gracious love and kindness toward me declared me not guilty.

Yes! I wanted restoration more than a good cup of coffee. Reading this scripture helped me to better understand why I need Jesus. Remember, I told you that early on in my life I left Jesus so far away from my life. Trying to live life without God the Father, the Lord Jesus Christ and the Holy Spirit was an effort in futility. Nothing in my life was successful until I made the decision to know God. His word gives me wisdom and draws me nearer to him daily; therefore, I go to the pallet again and again so that I can hear his instructions and listen as he teaches me how to live a life that is pleasing to him. I am grateful that he gave his precious blood to secure my salvation forever. He has made me right with him.

CHAPTER 3

A Safe Place

I sit here this morning and feel his divine presence. He reveals himself to me in a way that makes my heart burst with joy. Calmness overtakes my being as he speaks. You're probably asking, "Is this the only place you hear God?" Oh, let me tell you, it is not that I can't hear God in other rooms in my home, but I hear him crystal clear on the pallet. For now, it is our meeting place. He doesn't rush when he is talking, and I am so happy that he doesn't because I don't always get it the first time around. He is always patient with me and continues to teach me over and over until I get just what he is saying. Sometimes, my mind wanders all over the place but he gently brings me back to him. One morning, I had an *Ah-Ha* moment: The pallet is my safe place! Took me a minute but I got it. When he and I started this journey, he told me that *this is the place that the enemy could not get in*. That moment reminded me of the psalmist's confidence in Almighty God. He wrote, "He who dwells in the secret place of the Most High shall abide under the shadow of the Almighty. I will say of the Lord, he is my refuge and my fortress: my God in him will I trust." (Psalm 91:1-2) When I think of a fortress, I visualize a large, fortified building that keeps the enemy out. He is my safe place.

The Prayer Pallett

I completely belong to him. I know who Jesus is and what it means to seek him wholeheartedly. I accept his correction that moves my heart to obey and trust him. He has made it clear that I have free and immediate access to him; all I have to do is come. Unlike in times past, I now listen to him as he speaks in the scriptures. He gives me discernment and shows me those things that are not of him. He teaches me how to seek him when difficult situations arise. In him, I have hope, consolation, strength, and gratitude. What a blessed assurance to know that I have a safe place in Jesus, and that I am protected.

CHAPTER 4

Level of Discipline

Discipline was at the top of my priority list. I needed Godly discipline... plain and simple. The Spirit of God is so sensitive to our needs. I couldn't see that I needed self-control that only the Holy Spirit could give. I guess I saw what I wanted to see. Yet the Holy Spirit knew that my level of discipline was bordering on zero. He whispers to me ever so softly, "What's been trying to conquer you Ruth, you will be able to conquer it." Hallelujah!

God sits on the pallet and opens my mind to remember things that I learned years ago. Those things seemed right at the time, but my motives were so wrong. Needless to say, I didn't live up to the Word of God. If it wasn't for a Holy, all-knowing God, I would be nothing. When I faced God and told him to begin with me, I had a choice to listen, learn, and obey or continue to act foolishly. I remember reading the story in 1 Chronicles where David disobeyed God and conducted a census of Israel. Although his decision made God angry, God gave David three choices: 1) three years of famine; 2) three months of defeat by Israel's enemies; or 3) three days of deadly plague throughout Israel. Despite David's disobedience, he knew what he needed to do to return to right standing with God. David responded to God, "This is a terrible decision to make, but let me fall into the hands of the Lord rather than into the power of men, for God's mercies are very great." (I Chronicles 21:13).

Somehow, I understood David's petition. I had a choice. I could continue in my "feel good" style of living or I could choose God. Yep, you got it! I immediately chose God. I would rather for him to whip me than to leave me. I am in good hands with God. The Apostle Paul lays it out so clearly in Hebrews 12:11, "For the moment, all discipline seems painful rather than pleasant, but later it yields the peaceful fruit of righteousness to those who have been trained by it." What God is doing in my life right now may not feel good, but I am confident that I will reap the fruit of righteousness and peace. I, like David, know the greatness of God's mercies.

It is here that he gives me the power to conquer the things that have been conquering me. God is teaching me what I don't know and revealing to me things that I don't understand. I go to my pallet day after day expecting and listening to God. He's there! He shows up every time; therefore, I make myself available to spend time with him above all else. He is the answer to my problems and a very good listener.

James urged believers to be not only hearers of God's word but doers also; so, I have decided to obey God in all that I do to the best of my ability. I am learning the perfect law of God. You ask, "Ruth, what is He teaching you?" He is teaching me how to live His Word, to seek him with all my heart, and to remain steadfast in him.

I am desperate God! Everything else can wait. I just hope I'm not too late because he is all that matters. I am pursuing him like never before. Psalm 119:11 says, "I have stored up your word in my heart that I might not sin against you." The word of God will keep me from being blind and short-sighted in the things of God. I feel a cleansing taking place in my spirit, my heart, and my mind. 2 Peter 1:5-7 says, "For this very reason, make every effort to supplement your faith with virtue, and virtue with knowledge and knowledge with self-control and self-control with steadfastness and steadfastness with godliness and godliness with brotherly affection and brotherly affection with love."

I thought about the story of Zacchaeus in Luke 19:2-5. Zacchaeus was a chief tax collector who was rich because he swindled people out of their money through taxes. He wanted to know who this Jesus was, so he climbed a sycamore tree to get a good look as Jesus passed by. One more thing about this cheater was that he was a very short man....thus the tree. Zacchaeus wanted to look but Jesus had a different plan. Jesus looked up and told Zacchaeus to come down from the tree because he, Jesus, was going to visit his house today. Can you imagine being a cheater, but the Lord wants to eat at your house? The rest of the story...Zacchaeus hosted Jesus that day, received forgiveness, and accepted Christ as his Savior. Zacchaeus got more than he expected. I believe that deep within his spirit, he was desperate for Jesus. He just couldn't understand it until he came into Jesus' presence. This is the same with us. When we come into the presence of the living God, we receive more than we expect. When I lay prostrate before God on the pallet, I feel like Zacchaeus. I desperately need

Jesus. I need his word because just any old word won't do.

My time with God builds my faith so if I must stay on my pallet for hours on end, the value is for me. The relationship I want with God is on the pallet. I must go through the whole process for therein lies the value of discipline. My process is spending time with God so I can receive the discipline I need and desire. I want to know for myself that when I pass the test, I can move to another level in God.

CHAPTER 5

The Right Focus

As God brought me through the season of discipline, I realized that I can't go forward without having the right focus. I can be focused but if it is not the right focus, then I'm back at square one. Square one is definitely not where I need to be. I believe that right focus and discipline go hand in hand. The right focus is knowing that I can do absolutely nothing without Christ Jesus. Jesus makes it clear in John

15:5 (Amplified) "I am the Vine; you are the branches. The one who remains in Me and I in him bears much fruit, for [otherwise] apart from Me [that is, cut off from vital union with Me] you can do nothing." Nothing! That means not anything. I deliberately lived by my own rules before the pallet encounter. I was on my way to nowhere trying to live independently of the Jesus that I so desperately needed. Certainly, this self-proclaimed independence did not align with focusing on God and his will for my life.

The right focus is listening closely as he speaks and being obedient to what he tells me. I am face to face with the truth of the matter. My focus must be on developing an intimate relationship with Christ. It is deeper than saying I know him. It is not leaving him in the corner and going about my merry way. So, I listen intentionally (on purpose) and intently (eagerly) as he speaks to my heart. I sit quietly and listen closely as he tells me what he requires of me. He tells me to focus my mind habitually on heavenly things and not on earthly things which are temporary. Why? Because I died to this world and my new life is hidden with Christ in God. (Col. 3:2) Oh, but there is another part: When Christ, my life, appears then I will also appear with Him in glory. Then he tells me to seek first his kingdom and his righteousness, and all these things will be added unto me. (Matt. 6:33) I am obedient to every instruction that he gives me each time we meet on the pallet. The more I truly listen and obey, the more my attitude and my behavior change. I am clay in the potter's hands as he molds and shapes my life to please himself. If I don't understand what he tells me, I ask for clarification and understanding.

I recognize that the right focus has brought major benefits to my growth in Christ. First, he warns me and does not allow anything to sneak upon me. I can feel his presence when negative situations arise. I am not caught off guard, and he always assures me that he is with me. In fact, he gives me a sense of overwhelming peace. Second, no matter what the devil does to throw me off track, God keeps me safely in his arms. Third, I am discerning in my thoughts and actions. In other words, I think about what it is that God wants me to do, and I seek his guidance and understanding. Fourth, the Spirit of the Living God fills me and controls my heart, my mind, and my spirit. Fifth, my relationship is becoming more intimate with him as I seek him and obey him. Finally, my prayers are answered by God Almighty.

To God be the glory!

CHAPTER 6

Make God's Word Real

The word of God is one of the necessities that was missing in my life. I told you earlier, I lived by my own rules. I didn't have a clue of the true meaning of God's word. Yes, I knew the basics: the Lord's Prayer, the twenty-third Psalm, and maybe a couple more scriptures but I had no revelation or understanding of what they meant. As I started to read his word, I learned, "All scripture is breathed out by God and profitable for teaching, for reproof, for correction, and for training in righteousness, that the man of God may be competent, equipped for every good work." (2 Timothy 3:16-17). This one scripture says it all. Everything that I need is in the word of God. The author of Hebrews puts it this way: "God means what he says. What he says goes. His powerful Word is as sharp as a surgeon's scalpel, cutting through everything, whether doubt or defense, laying us open to listen and obey. Nothing and no one can resist God's Word. We can't get away from it—no matter what." (Heb. 4:12-13 Message Bible) This was just the beginning. I am obligated to read, to learn, to know, to obey, and to live his word, but how do I do this? Honestly, I don't know but the more I meet Jesus on the pallet, the more he teaches me about his word. The word of God is powerful, it sustains

The Prayer Pallett

me, and it is critical to my life. Psalm 119 clearly expresses that his word teaches, guides, directs, and leads us as he commands. I ask God for understanding and revelation as I read each verse slowly. It almost feels as though I'm learning to read for the first time. The more I read, the more I understand. One thing that I experienced is that I can read the same verse over and over and each time I learn a truth that I didn't read the time before.

Jesus is teaching me how my life can turn into a beautiful life of faithfulness in Christ Jesus. He lets me know that his power is present along with the solution to every problem that I encounter. I know now that I can trust God when I can't trace him. I receive joy and peace that saturates my innermost being. I can give my whole life and all that is connected to me to him. I am totally persuaded that Jesus is real. I am never ready to get out of his presence, but his Spirit prompts me to obey so when my heart fills up with the things of God each day, I want to share with others. The favor of God is working for me. When I receive all that God puts in my heart, there is nothing I can't do, nothing I can't say, and there is nothing I can't accomplish when I get my instructions from God. "For with God nothing shall be impossible." (Luke 1:37)

On my pallet, God gives me an open invitation to the throne room to come always and at any time. To know that an all-sovereign God is willing to hear my petitions at any time is more than I can sometimes comprehend. My spirit, my mind, and my body are being made whole. The covenant I have with God never expires. I am so grateful for a father that hears and answers prayers. He tells me, "Let us therefore come

The Prayer Pallett

boldly unto the throne of grace, that we may obtain mercy, and find grace to help in time of need. (Hebrews 4:16) It is good to reconcile back to him. Paul writes in Romans 5:10, "For if, when we were enemies, we were reconciled to God by the death of his Son, much more, being reconciled, we shall be saved by his life." When I go to him hungry and thirsty, I come back filled. When I long for something, my needs are met because as I learn, all of my answers are in him. I put on my listening ear, and he gets all of my attention. When there is a strong weariness on me, I am reminded, "Come unto me, all ye that labour and are heavy laden, and I will give you rest. Take my yoke upon you, and learn of me; for I am meek and lowly in heart: and ye shall find rest unto your souls. For my yoke is easy, and my burden is light. (Matthew 11:28-30). In the heat of what is going on in my life, God is becoming more and more real to me. I can depend on him for his loyalty because He never forgets me. His faithfulness keeps me standing firmly and speaking his promises.

    To God be the Glory!

CHAPTER 7

Vital to Christian Living

I spend more time on the pallet than I spend in my bed. Yes, this might sound funny, but it is the truth. My whole life is changing on this blue quilt. Again, I had no idea that a piece of fabric would usher in a completely new beginning for my life. Amazing!

There are times when my feelings and emotions take me in circles, and I feel as if I am on a spiritual roller coaster. One minute I'm believing I'm saved; the next minute I'm doubting I'm saved. Now we all know that faith and doubt cannot live together. It is either one or the other. I realize God is teaching me that salvation is not a feeling. I don't have to feel saved to be saved. I read Galatians 3:3 in which Paul writes to the church of Galatia, "How foolish can you be? After starting your new lives in the Spirit, why are you now trying to become perfect by your own human effort?" To me, the scripture is asking, "Ruth, are you trying to attain your goal by human effort?" No, no, no! I recognize that I cannot do anything on my own; therefore, I have no other choice but to stay before God. As a believer, I only need to embrace the change and stand on it! I AM SAVED!

I want to learn about and experience the work of the Spirit because I recognize that the Spirit is vital to my salvation and to my walk with God. I willingly surrender to the Holy Spirit and allow him to guide my life. I desire to live a Christ-centered life; not the life I lived before I truly met Jesus. I have learned that Jesus wants a relationship with me. He reminds me in John 15, "Abide in me and I will abide in you." As he continues to stay with me each day, I sit on the pallet with him and listen closely as he reveals more and more of himself. Not only am I learning who Jesus is, but I am also learning who I am in Jesus. Trust me, I didn't know before because I was doing my own thing. All that I am and all that I am not is revealed on the pallet and I understand fully that I owe it all to him. He teaches me his plan for my life and how I should live. As I listen, I desire to obey him. I am amazed at how he helps me to discern what is right and what is wrong. His voice is clear, and I no longer listen to stuff that frustrates me or to man's opinions.

I recognize that living a Christ-centered life is essential to my life. This reality is completely opposite to my old way of thinking and living. There is joy, peace, love and so much more to fill my life as I develop a relationship with Christ.

CHAPTER 8

Claim What is Mine

Passion, submission, humility, obedience, and relationship describe what I am feeling and experiencing as I sit on the pallet with my Father. These desires are totally opposite of what I experienced before I developed a deep longing for God. Where was I? What was I doing? WHAT WAS I THINKING? I wasn't. In this season, the Lord has revealed so much to me about my life and the importance and value of living a God-focused, Christ-centered, Holy Ghost-filled life. Now my focus is on pleasing and obeying him.

Early on, I admitted that the change had to begin with me. It wasn't going to come through osmosis or wishing it would happen. I have to be steadfast in my actions so I will continue what I have started, and I won't turn back. Now, I admit that it hasn't been easy. There have been days when I wanted to return to a few old habits. I listened to the negatives and sometimes felt they were more appealing than the positives that were taking place. However, in those seasons, I felt the Spirit guide me and talk to me. I listened and obeyed. As I sit here in quiet communion with Christ, I see the transformation in my thinking, my actions, my beliefs, my faith, and my desire. My entire being is changing. Hallelujah!

I don't have to make a deal with God because he knows my heart, my thoughts, and what I'm going to do. In fact, he knows me so it would be foolish to even try to think of a deal. However, what I know for sure is when I humble myself before God, there is nothing the enemy can throw at me and succeed. His word assures me in James 4:7, "So humble yourselves before God. Resist the devil and he will flee from you." As I surrender all to him, his mercy is always available to me. The thing about the word **all** is it includes everything without exception. I can't give him part of me, and I keep the other part. It doesn't work like that. So, I give him all of me and I am confident that his mercy is always available to me. Further, I don't have to be afraid because his protection always surrounds me.

I heard him say, "Ruth, where you are does not define where you're going.

My power and favor are operating in your life. I'm the One directing your path. I am preparing you to be the woman for the tasks that are before me as well as some unexpected ones!" Wow! How powerful! My current place is temporary because I am about to soar in his power. He is preparing me for greater. No, I don't know what it is, but I know with unwavering confidence that it is mighty. All I have to do is obey, walk in faith, and allow him to do the directing. He tells me in his word, "Trust in the Lord with all thine heart and lean not to thine own understanding. In all thy ways acknowledge him and he will direct thy path." (Prov. 3:5-6). I have learned that his plan for me is far greater than anything I could ever think of. Besides, if I think of something great, I can't do it in my own strength.

I claim all that he is promising me. The psalmist wrote in Psalm 37:4-5,

"Delight yourself in the Lord; and He will give you the desires of your heart. Commit your way to the Lord, trust also in Him, and He will do it." This scripture speaks to me because I want more of God. I long to grow closer and closer to him. There is so much more that I claim: healing, supernatural miracles, blessings, wisdom, and understanding.

And if the Lord is pleased with us, he will bring us safely into that land and give it to us. It is a rich land flowing with milk and honey. (Numbers 14:8)

CHAPTER 9

Sure To Win

On my pallet, God continuously reveals to me that to be in Christ Jesus, I must live in his will, listen to his voice, and obey him for he has a purpose for my life. He tells me in I Corinthians 2:9-10, "But as it is written, Eye hath not seen, nor ear heard, neither have entered into the heart of man, the things which God hath prepared for them that love him. But God hath revealed them unto us by his Spirit: for the Spirit searcheth all things, yea, the deep things of God." The Spirit softly whispers, "You are becoming a foe that the devil doesn't want to mess with. I am preparing you to be a light that will shine even in dark places. The attacks of Satan won't have any power over you because of what I'm putting within you, because of what I'm preparing you with, and where I'm taking you, he can't go. And if he comes, he can't stay. When Satan comes, he brings nothing but doubt, unbelief, and condemnation. Because of your obedience to me, he can't stick around. You are sure to win because of what you have inside of you. You are sure to win because you are learning how to fight back with the Word of God. You are learning how to stay within my will. You are quickly hearing what the Lord is saying and you are obeying." To God Be the Glory!

The Prayer Pallett

I quickly act on what I am learning. I am learning not to hold on to unforgiveness and to run away from ungodly stuff! God is whispering to me right now, "I am making you an overcomer. I'm giving you a new life because you choose to spend time with me. Because you spend time in my word and in prayer, I am strengthening you and enabling you to keep sin under your feet. I know you couldn't stay on the winning side by yourself. I appreciate you for asking for help. So as long as you listen to me and stay in a relationship with me, there will be no lack in your life because of the desire you have to live a new life. It can only be found in me."

> "A new heart also will I give you, and a new spirit will I put within you: and I will take away the stony heart out of your flesh, and

I will give you an heart of flesh. And I will put my spirit within you, and cause you to walk in my statutes, and ye shall keep my judgments, and do them." (Ezekiel 36:26-27)

Every day I experience how to live a life found only in Jesus Christ. Every day with him is sweeter than the day before. I have access to the power of God operating in my life. I have power through the Holy Spirit to subdue those old fleshly habits that hindered my walk with God. He has given me everything I need to live a new life. He teaches me to meditate on his word and to have faith in him. I'm sure to win because he is teaching me not to let fear conquer me. I can live free of fear and every time Satan comes against me, God lets me know that he has already provided a way of escape. I realize that the devil wants to see me fall flat on my face, but he doesn't know that it is hard to stumble when you are on your knees. I can beat him at his game. When it appears that there is no way out, when I'm in a jam and I'm backed against a wall, I put my trust in Jesus.

I am answering the call of God. I will live by his word. I am learning that he is not limited, and He can't be duplicated. He has given me a new heart and put his spirit within me. I am breaking away from what the devil is saying. I *will* live for Jesus.

On my pallet, he tells me to hold up my shield of faith so I can guard against all the fiery darts of the evil one no matter what situation I am in. Jesus opens my spiritual eyes to see Satan for what he is ...a liar! He has a strategy to take the word of God out of context and twist it into falsehoods. God's word tells us in Ephesians 6:10-11, "Finally, my brethren, be strong in the Lord and in the power of his might. Put on the whole armor of God that you may be able to stand against the wiles of the devil." The armor of God protects me from the schemes of the enemy. God had to explain to me the purpose of his armor and show me how to wear the *whole* armor to stand against the evil plans and tactics of the enemy. When I began this pallet journey, I had only one piece—the helmet of salvation but my one piece wasn't enough. I also need the belt of truth...personal integrity and moral courage; the breastplate of righteousness...an upright heart; the shoes of the gospel of peace...the good news of Christ; the shield of faith... steadfast reliance, unwavering confidence in God, his power, his goodness, and his love; the sword of the Spirit... God's word; and the power of prayer. You see, my strength is in God, and while the enemy might *try* to wreck my life, he will not succeed because he is under my feet, and I now know that he cannot stand against the armor of God. I am speaking the words of faith that God has poured into me each day of this journey on the prayer pallet. I am sure to win because of who lives in me, who I am, and whose I am.

To God Be the Glory!

Reference Page

All scripture references are taken from the:

The Message Bible
King James Version Bible
New King James Version Bible
Amplified Bible
New American Standard Bible
New English Translation

www.ingramcontent.com/pod-product-compliance
Lightning Source LLC
LaVergne TN
LVHW010612070526
838199LV00063BA/5145